**THIS GUIDE BELONGS TO**

**AS THEY PARENT**

*Date / Year*

# Kind Words from Parents, Grandparents, & Experts in Parenting

**Sandra Stanley**

Author of *Breathing Room*, and co-author of *Parenting: Getting it Right*, foster care advocate, mother of three

We all know where we want to end up in our parenting, but how to get there can seem like an unsolved mystery. The *Phase Guides* give us a resource to help out. They help to guide parents and caregivers through the different seasons of raising children, and provide a road map to parenting in such a way that we finish up with very few regrets.

### Sissy Goff M.Ed., LPC-MHSP

Co-director of Child and Adolescent Counseling at Daystar Counseling
Ministries, speaker and author of 12 books, including *Brave*

It's hard to connect with your child without first understanding where they
are. As counselors and speakers at parenting events across the country,
we spend a great deal of time teaching parents about development. To
know where your child is—not just physically, but emotionally, socially, and
spiritually, helps you to truly know and understand who your child is. And
that understanding is the key to connecting.

The *Phase Guides* give you the tools to do just that. Through the research
of the Phase Project, *Phase Guides* are an insightful, hopeful, practical, and
literal year-by-year guide that will help you to understand and connect with
your child at every age.

### Jennifer Walker, RN BSN

Author and co-founder of Moms On Call, mother of three

These resources for parents are fantastically empowering, absolute in their
simplicity, and completely doable in every way. The hard work that has gone
into the Phase Project will echo through the next generation of children in
powerful ways.

### Tina Naidoo

Executive Director of The Potter's House of Dallas, Inc

It's true that parenting is one of life's greatest joys but it is not without
its challenges. If we're honest, parenting can sometimes feel like trying
to choreograph a dance to an ever-changing beat. It can be clumsy and
riddled with well-meaning missteps. If parenting is a dance, this *Phase
Guide* is a skilled instructor refining your technique and helping you move
gracefully to a steady beat.

For those of us who love to plan ahead, this guide will help you anticipate
what's to come so you can be poised and ready to embrace the moments you
want to enjoy.

### Carlos Whittaker

Speaker, storyteller, best-selling author of multiple books, including *How to Human*, father of three

Not only are the *Phase Guides* the most creative and well-thought-out guides to parenting I have ever encountered, these books are essential to my daily parenting.

With three kids of my own, I know what it's like to swim in the wake of daily drama and delicacy. These books are a reminder to enjoy every second. Because it's just a phase.

### Cheryl Jackson

Founder of Minnie's Food Pantry, award-winning philanthropist, grandmother

As the founder of Minnie's Food Pantry, I see thousands of people each month with children who will benefit from the advice, guidance, and nuggets of information on how to celebrate and understand the phases of their child's life.

Too often we feel like we're losing our mind when sweet little Johnny starts to change his behavior into a person we do not know. I can't wait to start implementing the principles of these books with my clients to remind them... it's just a phase.

### David Thomas, LMSW

Co-director of Family Counseling, Daystar Counseling Ministries, speaker, and author of 10 Books including *Wild Things: The Art of Nurturing Boys*, father of three

I began exploring this resource with my counselor hat on, thinking how valuable this will be for the many parents I spend time with in my office. I ended up taking my counselor hat off and putting on my parent hat. Then I kept thinking about friends who are teachers, coaches, youth pastors, and children's ministers, who would want this in their hands.

What a valuable resource the Orange team has given us to better understand and care for the kids and adolescents we love. I look forward to sharing it broadly.

### Josh Shipp

Best-selling author of *The Grown-Up's Guide to Teenage Humans*, award-winning speaker, teen expert, father of three

As I speak to high school students and their parents, I always wonder to myself: What would it have been like if they had better seen what was coming next? What if they had a guide that would tell them what to expect and how to be ready? What if they could anticipate what is predictable about the high school years before they actually hit?

These *Phase Guides* give a parent that kind of preparation so they can have a plan when they need it most.

### Danielle Strickland

Speaker, global social activist, author of *The Other Side of Hope*, mother of three

The *Phase Guides* are incredibly creative, well researched, and filled with inspirational actions for everyday life. Each age-specific guide is catalytic for equipping parents to lead and love their kids as they grow up.

I'm blown away and deeply encouraged by the content and by its creators. I highly recommend Phase resources for all parents, teachers, and influencers of children. This is the stuff that challenges us and changes our world. Get them. Read them. And use them!

### Courtney DeFeo

Author of *Treasured* and *In This House* and *We Will Giggle*, podcaster, mother of two

I have always wished someone would hand me a manual for parenting. Well, the *Phase Guides* are more than what I wished for. They guide, inspire, and challenge me as a parent—while giving me incredible insight into my children at each age and phase. Our family will be using these every year!

# Parenting Your One-Year-Old

## A GUIDE TO MAKING THE MOST OF THE "I CAN DO IT" PHASE

**THE PHASE PROJECT**

**Parenting Your One-Year-Old:**
**A Guide to Making the Most of the**
**"I Can Do It" Phase**

Published by Orange, a division of The reThink Group, Inc.,
5870 Charlotte Lane, Suite 300, Cumming, GA 30040 U.S.A.

Parent Cue ® is a registered trademark of The reThink Group, Inc.
It's Just a Phase ® is a registered trademark of The Phase Project, LLC.



ISBN: 978-1-63570-214-9
© 2024 The Phase Project, LLC

Printed in United States of America
Second Edition 2024
1 2 3 4 5 6 7 8 9 10
06/01/2024

*Special thanks to —*

**JON ACUFF** for guidance and consultation on having conversations about technological responsibility

**JIM BURNS, PH.D** for guidance and consultation on having conversations about sexual integrity

**JEAN SUMNER, MD** for guidance and consultation on having conversations about healthy habits

**CHINWÉ WILLIAMS, PH.D** for guidance and consultation on how to navigate crisis

Every educator, counselor, community leader, and researcher who invested in the Phase Project

**In Partnership →**

Parent Cue partners with the Phase Project, designing Phase Guides to help you parent your child through every year in the four main phases: Preschool, Elementary School, Middle School, and High School.

**The Phase Project →**

Started in 2013, the Phase Project is a synthesis of personal experience, academic research, and gatherings of leaders and educational experts from across the child development spectrum.

# Contents

# How to Use This Guide



**The guide you hold in your hand doesn't have very many words, but it does have a lot of ideas.**

Some of these ideas come from thousands of hours of research. Others come from parents, educators, and volunteers who spend every day with kids the same age as yours. This guide won't tell you everything about your kid, but it will tell you a few things about kids at this age.

The best way to use this guide is to take what these pages tell you about one-year-olds and combine it with what you know is true about your one-year-old.

After each idea in this guide, there are pages with a few questions designed to prompt you to think about your kid, your family, and yourself as a parent. The only guarantee we give to parents who use this guide is this: You will mess up some things as a parent this year. Actually, that's a guarantee to every parent, regardless. But you, you picked up this book!

You want to be a better parent. And that's what we hope this guide will do: help you parent your toddler just a little better, simply because you paused to consider a few ideas that can help you make the most of this phase.

# Let's sum it up:

Things about one-year-olds

+

Thoughts about <u>your</u> one-year-old

=

Your guide to the next 52 weeks of parenting

**Dear Parent,**

# Welcome to a new phase!

**I'M NOT SURE WHAT CAPTIVATES ME MORE...** the spontaneous belly laugh or the drool-mouthed wonder on their angelic faces. I can fall in love with a one-year-old faster than they can stink up a room with a saggy diaper. The cherub cheeks and adorably fat thighs draw me in, almost enough to make me overlook their incessantly snotty nose and the jelly they just smeared in their wispy new-grown hair. Almost.

It's the mess that gets me. Their little fingers are drawn like magnets to anything they can break or mangle. The moment their hands become sticky-gooey, an internal signal screams somewhere in their little bodies, "Wipe yourself on something clean and white. Right now!"

Sitting at the dinner table, I see the same look on my granddaughter Mollie's face that I saw on her daddy's face so many years ago. It's the look of curiosity that drives a toddler to snatch and smear, squish, then shriek with delight. I glance across to see the look on her mom's face. It reads: Could I just eat a meal without being completely grossed out, maybe while the food is still reasonably warm?

It's hard to believe, but yes, that day will come. But not until Mollie has discovered how much pasta her ears will hold or what a bowl of applesauce feels like as it drips down her face, neck, and eventually… to the floor.

Sweet discovery is what this phase is made of. It's what makes patience and endurance such prized commodities for the parents of this age. You are helping your one-year-old navigate the mess of discovery.

During this phase, your brilliant bundle of exhaustless energy will climb her first stairs, say her first sentence, and begin to test her independence—independence that will be illustrated with piercing shrieks, and that vehemently spoken word: "No!"

But within the mess is an indescribable joy. He just toddled his first Frankenstein steps, three in a row, boasting the proud look of an astronaut landing on the moon. She just grabbed a crayon and scribbled her first work of art. Your darling can identify his nose and eyes and ears on command (to rousing applause), and you are certain he has the makings of a brain surgeon.

Sweet joy and pride so big it hurts—this is what wells up in the hearts of moms and dads as they watch their one-year-old develop into a little person with opinions and intellect and personality. And as you gaze, you begin to realize what this really means. Not only do you get a ringside seat to watch the beauty of potential form right before your eyes, but you get the joy of helping influence, train, and build who your child will become. Just remember: There will come a day when your once-helpless baby will bathe, dress, and feed himself, but the journey to get there comes with a little mess along the way.

## Sherry Surratt

*Former president and CEO of MOPS International, speaker, author, and grandmother*

# 52 Weeks to Parent Your One-Year-Old

WHEN YOU SEE
HOW MUCH TIME
YOU HAVE LEFT,
YOU TEND TO DO
MORE WITH
THE TIME YOU
HAVE NOW.

# For some, this phase sounds like...

# There are approximately 936 weeks from the time a baby is born until they grow up and move to whatever is next.

It may seem hard to believe, but <u>at least 52 of those weeks have already passed you by</u>. And, while the future still feels far away, you're probably beginning to realize that your baby is growing up faster than you ever dreamed.

That's why every week counts. Of course, each week on its own might not feel significant. There may be weeks this year when you feel like all you've accomplished was translating toddler babble. That's okay.

Take a deep breath. You don't have to get everything done this week.

But what happens in your child's life week after week, year after year, adds up over time. So, it might be a good idea to put a number to your weeks.

## Measure It Out

**HINT:**

*If you want a little help counting it out, you can download the free Parent Cue app on all mobile platforms.*

Write down the number of weeks that have already passed since your one-year-old was born. Then write down the number of weeks you have left before they graduate high school.

*Write down the number.*



## Create a Visual Countdown

Find a jar and fill it with one marble for each week you have remaining with your child. Then make a habit of removing one marble every week as a reminder to make the most of your time.

*Where can you place your visual countdown so you will see it frequently?*

*Which day of the week is best for you to remove a marble?*

*Is there anything you want to do each week as you remove a marble?*

HINT:

*Say a prayer, write in a baby book, retell one favorite memory from this past week.*

*Bonus idea— place the marble you removed into a second jar so you can see how much time you've invested in your child.*

# You only have <u>52 weeks</u> with your one-year-old while they are still one.



Then they will be two, and you will never know them as a one-year-old again. That might be incredibly emotional, or it might be the best news you've heard all day.

Or to say it another way:

> **Before you know it, your toddler will grow up a little more and...**
> → **be potty trained.**
> → **speak in sentences.**
> → **dress themselves.**

Just remember, the phase you are in now has remarkable potential. Before their second birthday, there are some distinctive opportunities you don't want to miss.

So, as you count down the next 52 weeks, pay attention to what makes these weeks different from the rest of the weeks you will have with your child as they grow.

# EVERY PHASE IS A TIMEFRAME IN A KID OR TEENAGER'S LIFE WHEN YOU CAN LEVERAGE DISTINCTIVE OPPORTUNITIES TO INFLUENCE THEIR FUTURE.

# Reflect

*What are some things you have noticed about your one-year-old in this phase that you really enjoy?*

*What is something new you are learning as a parent during this phase?*

# The phase when nobody's on time, everything's a mess, and one eager toddler will insist, "I can do it."

### Expect to be late.

Maybe you had to wait for your toddler to "do it myself" (just try and stop them). Or maybe they impressively filled a clean diaper just as you got into the car. Whatever the reason, this phase will make even the most punctual adult miss the mark occasionally.

### Look forward to a few fashion statements.

Expect a few mismatched outfits, magic marker tattoos, sticker collages, and other various states of creative expression. In this phase, you will choose not only your battles, but also which messes will just have to be tolerated.

### Their struggle for independence has begun.

You feel it the first time they try to feed themselves and dump applesauce down the front of their shirt. Just remember, by letting them do some things "myself," they're not only learning new skills, they're also developing the confidence they need in order to move to the next phase.

# Every one-year-old is unique.

DISCOVER THIS PHASE

Even with unique one-year-olds—which yours most certainly is—most one-year-olds have a few things in common. This book will show you what those are so you can make the most of the "I Can Do It" Phase.

*Remember: We haven't met <u>your</u> one-year-old. This book is just about a lot of one-year-olds.*

Some may still be working on their first words.

Some will never. Stop. Talking.

Some may prefer to smear their diapers on the wall.

Some will always poop in the big toilet.

Some will happily eat quinoa and artichokes.

Some will go on hunger strike if it's not a chicken nugget.

Some will remove their socks and shoes in eleven seconds flat.

Some will model cute hats all day long.

Some take a two-hour nap every afternoon.

Some have to be barricaded in their room for a ten-minute quiet time.

Some can climb up and down the stairs without help.

Some are climbing up the walls.

Some may craft amazing shapes from Play-Doh.®

Some may eat the Play-Doh.® (Okay, so we're pretty sure all of them do that.)

# This year,
# your one-year-old
# is changing.

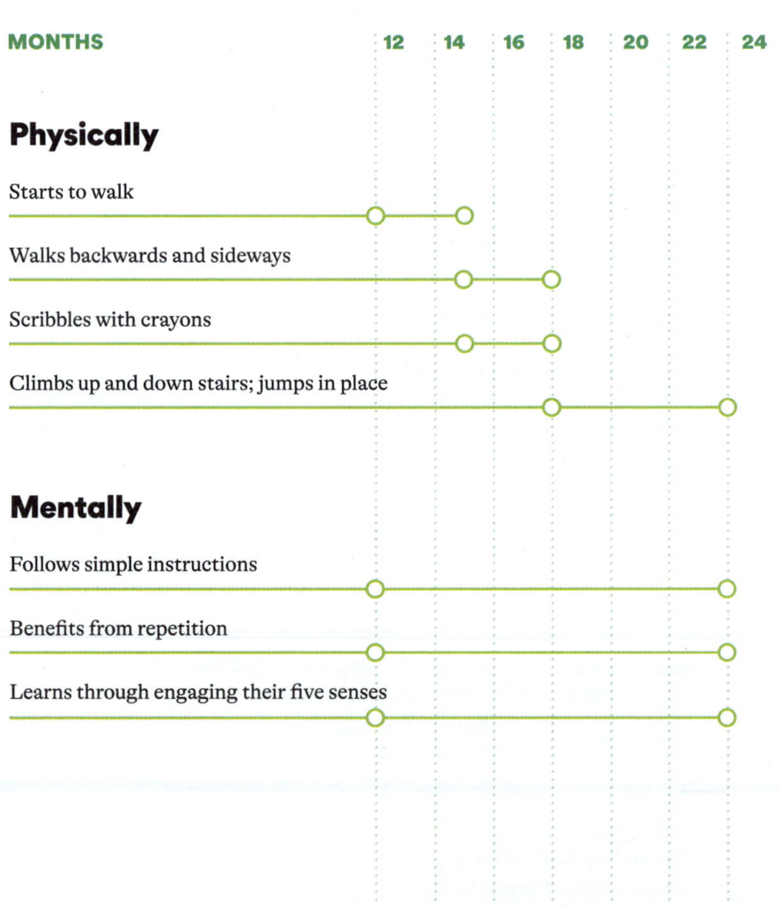

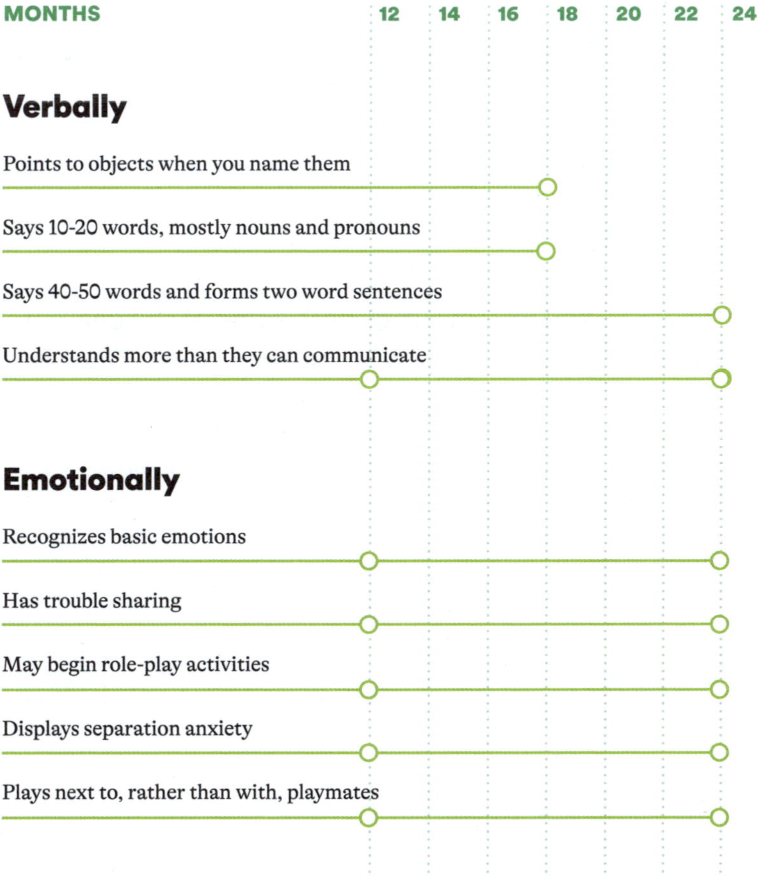

| MONTHS | 12 | 14 | 16 | 18 | 20 | 22 | 24 |
|---|---|---|---|---|---|---|---|

## Verbally

Points to objects when you name them

Says 10-20 words, mostly nouns and pronouns

Says 40-50 words and forms two word sentences

Understands more than they can communicate

## Emotionally

Recognizes basic emotions

Has trouble sharing

May begin role-play activities

Displays separation anxiety

Plays next to, rather than with, playmates

*What are some changes you are noticing in your one-year-old?*



You may disagree with some of the characteristics we've shared about one-year-olds. That's because every one-year-old is unique.

*What makes your one-year-old different from one-year-olds in general?*

*What do you want to remember about this year with your one-year-old?*

## SECTION 1.    DISCOVER

# First Steps

When your baby walks for the first time, your whole world will change. Here are some things to get ready for:

**Be patient.** Your baby will walk when she is ready, so don't pressure her too much. Walking only makes babies faster and harder to chase. (Most babies will walk between 12-15 months.)

**Signs your baby may be ready to walk.**
→ Pulling up to stand
→ Standing while playing
→ Standing without support

**Make your home safe to explore.** Consider what a toddler might have easier access to, what you need to put away, and where you might want to install safety gates. Cushion any sharp edges.

**Cheer for them.** Cheers will automatically erupt when your baby walks his first steps. Continue to praise him even when he falls, and encourage him to get right back up.

**Celebrate the moment.** Capture the moment with pictures or video, even if you have to recreate the moment later. First steps will be adorably wobbly for days.

# Reflect

Walking changes the game for your baby.

*What do you need to do to get your home ready?*

*Write down a few memories to share with your kid later about their first steps, including the date.*

2

# Six Things Every Kid Needs

WHEN YOU SEE HOW MUCH TIME YOU HAVE LEFT, YOU TEND TO MAKE WHAT MATTERS, MATTER MORE.

# It's worth repeating: When you see how much time you have left, you tend to make what matters, matter more.

Depending on your personality, that can sound empowering, or just like a lot of pressure. Relax. Every day doesn't have to create a memory worth posting.

The important thing to remember is a countdown clock doesn't mean you try to squeeze more things into each week so you can get the most out of it. It actually means acknowledging that you can't do what you can't do.

You can't make your toddler always behave in public. But over time you can show them the kind of love that is the foundation for how we treat each other.

You can't make your toddler make wise choices. But over time you can introduce them to stories that widen their perspective and inform their decision-making.

You can't make your toddler be a good friend. But you can give them safe places to belong so they will know that people matter.

You can't make your toddler perform at the top of their class. But you can make learning fun, and use mistakes as opportunities to grow.

This week matters because it's an opportunity to give your toddler a few things that really matter. You can't do what you can't do. Let some things go, and you might just discover you're already doing more significant things than you ever realized.

# Your kid needs six things over time.

Over the next 884 weeks, your child will need many things.

Some of the things your kid needs will change from phase to phase, but there are six things that every kid needs at every phase. In fact, these things may be the most important things you give your kid—other than food. Kids need food.

The next few pages are designed to help you think about how you can give these things to your one-year-old—before they turn two.

# Every kid, at every phase, needs:

 **Love** to give them a sense of *worth*.

 **Stories** to give them a bigger *perspective*.

 **Work** to give them *purpose*.

 **Fun** to give them *connection*.

 **People** to give them *belonging*.

 **Words** to give them *direction*.

**No. 1**

# Every kid needs **love** over time to give them a sense of **worth.**

## One question your one-year-old is asking:

Your toddler's changing ability is a crisis—for you, and for them. This is a season filled with uncertainty, imperfection, and even failure as they struggle to keep up with all their newly developing skills. Your one-year-old is asking one major question: **"Am I able?"**

As the parent of a one-year-old who may scream more than you imagined, sleep less than you had hoped, or make more messes than you thought possible, you may feel overwhelmed at times. But remember this—in order to give your one-year-old the love they need, you only need to do one thing: **Embrace their physical needs.**

> When you embrace your one-year-old's physical needs, you...
> ① communicate that they are safe,
> ② establish that the world can be trusted, and
> ③ demonstrate that they are worth loving.

# Reflect

You are probably doing more than you realize to show your one-year-old just how much you love them.

*Make a list of the ways you already show up consistently to embrace your one-year-old's physical needs.*

# Showing love requires paying attention to what someone likes.

*What does your one-year-old seem to enjoy the most right now?*

It's impossible to love anyone with the relentless effort a one-year-old demands unless you have a little time for yourself.

*What can you do to refuel each week so you are able to give your one-year-old the love they need?*

*Who do you have around you supporting you this year?*

**No. 2**

# Every kid needs **stories** over time to give them a bigger **perspective.**

## Books to read with your one-year-old:

Whose Knees Are These
*by Jabari Asim*

Inside Outside Upside Down
*by Stan and Jan Berenstain*

Blue Hat, Green Hat
*by Sandra Boynton*

Opposites
*by Sandra Boynton*

The Runaway Bunny
*by Margaret Wise Brown*

Five Little Monkeys Jumping on the Bed
*by Eileen Christelow*

Full, Full, Full of Love
*by Trish Cooke*

Freight Train
*by Donald Crews*

Click, Clack, Moo, Cows That Type
*by Doreen Cronin*

Are You My Mother?
*by P.D. Eastman*

Go, Dog. Go!
*by P.D. Eastman*

Shh! We Have a Plan
*by Chris Haughton*

Can I Have a Pet
*by Gwendolyn Hudson Hooks*

Peekaboo Morning
*by Rachel Isadora*

Whistle for Willie
*by Ezra Jack Keats*

Sheep in a Jeep
*by Nancy E Shaw*

Caps for Sale
*by Esphyr Slobodkina*

Let's Dance
*by Valerie Bolling*

**HINT:**

*You can find a more in-depth reading list at ParentCue.org.*

# Reflect

Kids need the kind of stories you will read to them over time. But they also need family stories.

*What can you do this year to capture your family's story so you can retell the story of this year to your one-year-old when they are older?*

*What makes your family history unique? How can you preserve the story of your family's history for your one-year-old?*

*Are there other stories that matter to you? What are they, and how will you share those stories with your toddler?*

## SECTION 2.    STORIES

**No. 3**

# Every kid needs **work** over time to give them **purpose.**

# Work your one-year-old can do:

→

Walk

Pick up a toy and put it away

Hold a sippy cup

Drink from a straw

Take trash to the trash can

Follow one-step instructions *(like, "Hand it to me.")*

Help fill a pet's food dish

Feed themselves

Help as you dress them *(by not running away)*

Undress themselves

Clean up spills *(or spread the water around on the floor)*

# Reflect

*What are some things your one-year-old has worked to accomplish so far?*

# Letting your one-year-old "do it myself" takes patience— and a lot of wet wipes.

*How are you allowing for extra time for your one-year-old to try new things? What do you do to reward their efforts?*

*What are some things you hope your one-year-old will be able to do independently in the next phase?*

*How are you helping your one-year-old develop those skills now?*

**No. 4**

# Every kid needs **fun** over time to give them **connection.**

# Ways to have fun with your one-year-old:

## Toys

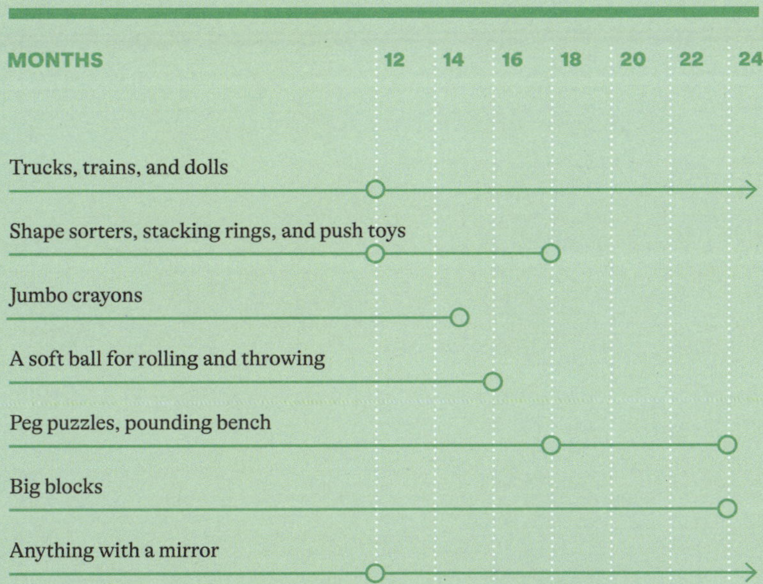


## Activities

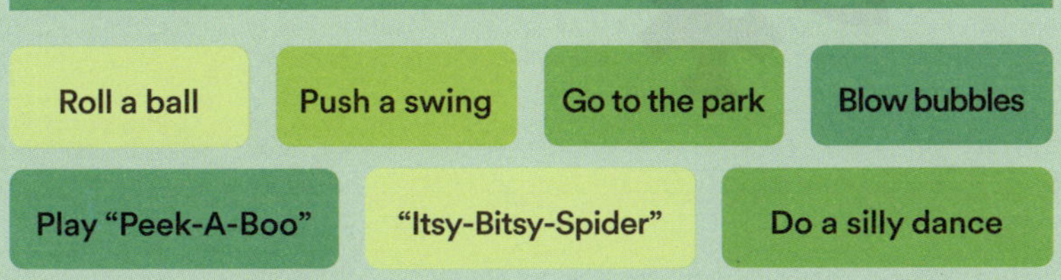

# Reflect

*What are some activities that make you and your one-year-old laugh?*

*When are the best times of the day, or week, for you to set aside to have fun with your one-year-old?*

*What are some ways you want to celebrate the special days coming up this year?*

## Second Birthday

# Holidays

**No. 5**

# Every kid needs **people** over time to give them **belonging.**

## Adults who might influence your one-year-old:

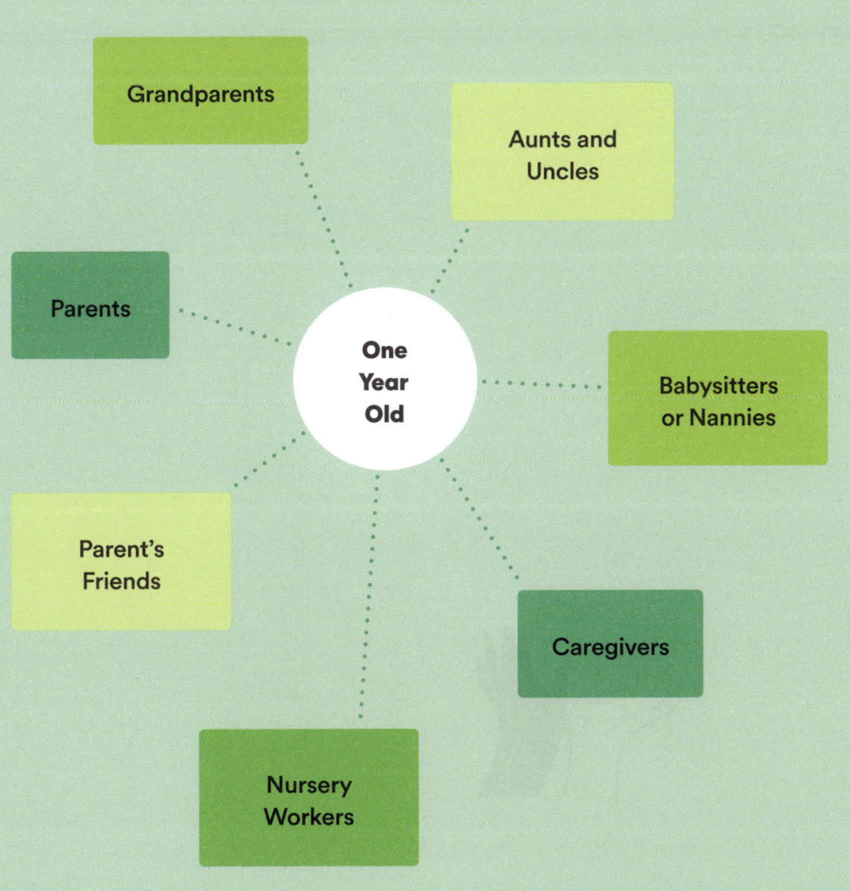

# Reflect



*List at least five adults who have influence in your one-year-old's life right now.*

*What is one way these adults could help you and your one-year-old this year?*

*What are a few ways you could show these adults appreciation for the significant role they play in your child's life?*

## SECTION 2.    PEOPLE

**No. 6**

# Every kid needs **words** over time to give them **direction.**

## Words your one-year-old needs to hear:

Improving your child's vocabulary will help them in the phases to come. Here are a few ways you can help:

① Talk to your toddler—the more, the better.
② Repeat what they say, and add words. (When they say "truck," you say, "Would you like to play with your truck?")
③ Make eye contact.
④ Point at objects when you name them.

# Reflect

*What word (or words) describe your hopes for your one-year-old in this phase?*



| | | |
|---|---|---|
| Determined | Motivated | Gentle |
| Encouraging | Introspective | Passionate |
| Self-Assured | Enthusiastic | Patient |
| Assertive | Joyful | Forgiving |
| Daring | Entertaining | Creative |
| Insightful | Independent | Witty |
| Compassionate | Observant | Ambitious |
| Amiable | Sensitive | Helpful |
| Easy-Going | Endearing | Authentic |
| Diligent | Adventurous | Inventive |
| Proactive | Honest | Devoted |
| Optimistic | Curious | Genuine |
| Fearless | Dependable | Attentive |
| Affectionate | Generous | Harmonious |
| Courageous | Committed | Empathetic |
| Cautious | Responsible | Courageous |
| Devoted | Trustworthy | Flexible |
| Inquisitive | Thoughtful | Careful |
| Patient | Loyal | Nurturing |
| Open-minded | Kind | Reliable |

*Where can you place those words in your home so they will remind you what you want for your one-year-old this year?*

# One-year-olds may say up to 50 words before their second birthday.



**HINT:**

*At some point this year, try to get a recording of their voice—it will have changed before you know it.*

*Write down some of your one-year-old's first and favorite words.*

JOURNAL

**SECTION 2.    WORDS**

# WHEN YOU SEE HOW MUCH TIME YOU HAVE LEFT, YOU TEND TO VALUE WHAT HAPPENS OVER TIME.

**The most important things we give our kids aren't the gifts we just give once, but the ones we give over time. Just remember...**

We don't experience worth because we are loved once, but because we are **loved** by someone over time.

We don't understand the world through a single event, but through a collection of **stories** over time.

We don't usually discover our purpose in one great revelation, but through consistent opportunities to **work** over time.

We don't develop trusted relationships in a day, but we become connected to others through laughter, **fun**, and shared experiences over time.

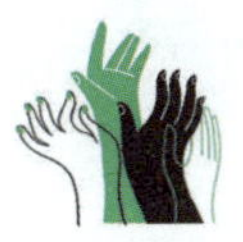

We don't know we belong because of a single invitation, but because we have been welcomed by **people** over time.

We are not motivated to action by one statement, but by **words** that move us over time.

# Four Conversations to Have in this Phase

WHEN YOU KNOW WHERE YOU WANT TO GO, AND YOU KNOW WHERE YOU ARE NOW, YOU CAN ALWAYS DO SOMETHING TO MOVE IN A BETTER DIRECTION.

# Over the next 884 weeks of your child's life, some conversations may matter more than others.

What you say, for example, regarding
**pirates, spiders, and football**
might have less impact on their future
than what you say regarding
**health, sex, technology, or faith.**

The next pages are about the conversations that matter most. On the left page is a destination—what you might want to be true in your kid's life 884 weeks from now. On the right page is a goal for conversations with your one-year-old and a few suggestions about what you might want to say.

# Healthy Habits

## Learning to strengthen my body through exercise, nutrition, and self-advocacy

01 / 04

This year you will establish basic nutrition so your child will have consistent care and experience a variety of food.

Your one-year-old understands the world better when you talk about what you're doing as you do it. So build a foundation for healthy habits by repeating a few simple phrases this year…

## Say things like...

Today, we're going to see Doctor Mark.

"Can you show me where it hurts?"

It's nap time.

Yum! It's green beans!

Let's go outside.

Let's wash your hands.

# Reflect



**HINT:**

*Okay, "exercise" may be a stretch, but running after big kids at the park counts.*

*What are your goals for providing your one-year-old with good nutrition and exercise?*

*Who will help you monitor and improve your one-year-old's health this year?*

*What are your own health goals for this year? How can you improve the habits in your own life—even in a phase when your most common health question might be, "Should I use their nap time to sleep or shower or eat?"*

## SECTION 3.    HEALTH

# Sexual Integrity

## Guarding my potential for intimacy through appropriate boundaries and mutual respect



This year you will introduce them to their body so your child will discover their body and define privacy.

Your conversations with your one-year-old regarding sexual integrity will never be simpler than they are right now. But it's never too early to start with some of the right words.

## Say things like...



Help your child learn the correct names of body parts—experts suggest that learning proper words can protect your kid from potential harm as well as create a positive view of their body.

# Reflect



**HINT:**

*Parents,
media, friends,
other adults…*

*What influences shaped your views of sex growing up?*

*How does your own life story shape your future hopes for your child in this area?*

*When it comes to your child's sexuality, what do you hope is true for them 884 weeks from now?*

*Are you and your spouse, or your child's other parent, on the same page when it comes to talking about sex with your child?*

*How might you work on a plan to communicate your hopes and expectations about sex through real-time conversations with your child?*

# Technological Responsibility

## Leveraging the potential of online experiences to enhance my offline community and success

This year you will enjoy the advantages so your child will experience boundaries and have positive exposure.

Every one-year-old is eager to discover the magical screen with lights and buttons. Even though there's definitely such a thing as too much screen time, technology does have a few benefits for you and your one-year-old. So start having a few conversations about the digital devices in your home.

## Say things like...

Look at you!

Take as many photos as you like.
You will enjoy seeing them later.

A phone is not a hammer.

Tablets don't go in the bathtub.

No juice by the
computer.

Let's turn off the TV now.

One-year-olds don't need to watch a full season
of *Sesame Street* in one sitting.

# Reflect

*What kind of digital access was available to you when you were growing up? How have things changed since then?*

*What are some issues you think may come up as you raise your one-year-old in a digitally connected world? Where can you go to find advice to help navigate those issues?*

*When it comes to your child's engagement with technology, what do you hope is true for them 884 weeks from now?*

*What are your own personal values and disciplines when it comes to leveraging technology? Are there ways you want to improve your own savvy, skill, or responsibility in this area?*

# Authentic Faith

## Trusting Jesus in a way that transforms how I love God, myself, and the rest of the world

This year you will <u>incite wonder</u> so your child will know God's love and meet God's family.

Your one-year-old listens to your words. So this phase is the perfect time to begin talking, singing, and praying together with your toddler. Begin by simply incorporating faith into your daily routines.

04 / 04

## Say things like...

God made you. God loves you.
Jesus wants to be your friend forever.

God, thank You for...
God, please help us...

Pray aloud while you are with
your one-year-old.

Jesus loves me.

Sing songs together.

Let's go to church!

Connect with a faith community.

# Reflect

*Who will help you develop your child's faith as they grow?*

*Is there a volunteer at your church who shows up consistently each week for your child? Do you attend a consistent service so your one-year-old knows who will greet them each week?*

*When it comes to your child's faith, what do you hope is true for them 884 weeks from now?*

*What routines or habits do you have in your own life that are stretching your faith?*

# Rhythms and Responses

# The rhythm of your week will shape the values in your home.



Now that you have filled this book with dreams, ideas, and goals, it may seem as if you will never have time to get it all done. Actually, you have 884 weeks. And every week has potential.

The secret to making the most of this phase with your one-year-old is to take advantage of the time you already have. Create a rhythm to your weeks by leveraging these four times together.

## Morning Time

Set the mood for the day. Smile. Greet them with words of love.

## Drive Time

Reinforce simple ideas. Talk to your toddler and play music as you go.

## Cuddle Time

Be personal. Spend one-on-one time that communicates love and affection.

## Bath Time

Wind down together. Provide comfort as the day draws to a close.

# Reflect

*What seem to be your one-year-old's best times of the day?*

*What are some of your favorite routines with your one-year-old?*

*Write down any other thoughts or questions that you have about parenting your one-year-old.*

## SECTION 4.    CUE TIMES

# Preparing for the Unexpected

## Parenting humans at any phase of life is filled with the unexpected.

No matter the age, sometimes the unexpected discoveries we make as parents may elicit fear, anger, or confusion as we try to guide our kid toward a positive future. It may even be something that is completely out of our control, like a medical diagnosis or a family tragedy. That's why it's best to create a response plan when you are clear and thoughtful.

So, take a few, deep breaths. Find a place where you feel safe and comfortable. If you need to walk away and come back to this at a later time, that's okay, too.

**Download → parentcue.org/preparing**

# Reflect

Every parent has what it takes to navigate challenges with their kids, but none of us can carry the weight alone.

**HINT:**

*Think of someone with whom you feel safe enough to be completely honest about what is happening and what you are feeling.*

*If you were to discover something you weren't expecting in your kid's life, who would you be able to call?*

*How would you begin that conversation?*

Every kid who is navigating challenging situations needs their parent's involvement. But a parent may not be the only influence they need.

*If you were to discover something you weren't expecting, who else in your kid's life could you count on to walk with them through this experience?*



*What might you want to go ahead and share with them about your kid and/ or your family?*

# Navigating Crisis

## What is a crisis?

A crisis is any real or perceived threat to your child. And it's inevitable. Even though you are a great parent, you won't be able to protect your child from some pain during their toddler years. There is a wide range of events that classify as "crisis" ranging from temporary to long-term and from mild to severe.

## How do you recognize it?

Just because your toddler may not know how to talk about it doesn't mean they are unaffected. Watch for these three things:

### ① Are they regressing?

During a crisis, toddlers will often try to take more control of their world by regressing in potty training, verbal skills, motor development, or behavior.

### ② How are they playing?

As your toddler plays with toys, listen to the conversations the toys have with each other and watch how the toys treat each other.

### ③ What are they drawing?

Toddlers may begin to draw what they are processing. Asking your child about their drawings will give you insight into their mind and heart.

## How do you respond to it?

### ① Re-establish some routine.

Toddlers love predictability. Talk to them about changes in their routine while reminding them what has stayed the same. Establish new expectations and a new routine.

### ② Play with them.

If you notice something in your child's play, join them. Thirty minutes of one-on-one play with your child establishes a meaningful connection, which helps them feel safe.

### ③ Make music.

Music is healing. It's multi-sensory, non-threatening, structured, personalized, fun, and accessible.

### ④ Respect their boundaries.

When offering affection, model and respect their boundaries by asking, "Would you like me to hold you?" "Do you want a hug?" Your toddler may need a safe space alone to process their emotions first.

### ⑤ Answer their questions.

Listen first. Paraphrase their words to make sure you understand their question and concern. Then, give an honest answer in a calm, reassuring voice, using as few words as possible.

⑥ **Take care of yourself.**

When your toddler is in crisis, you may be in crisis as well. Seek care. Find community. Take some personal time. This may be the best thing you can do to help your child.

⑦ **Get outside help.**

Consider if your toddler is being hurt by someone, hurting others, or hurting themselves. Or if you are also hurting and not currently able to provide support.

# What's Next: The Two-Year-Old Phase

# In only 52 weeks you will rediscover your toddler as a two-year-old.

One of the joys of parenting is the many surprises that greet you around every corner.

We can't prepare you for all the joys that await you in the next phase, but we can give you a glimpse of a few things that might help you anticipate what's coming.

## The two-year-old phase may look like...

*Temper tantrums*

Getting tickled back

*Art... made with or on something unexpected*

Letting them do things by themselves you wish you could do yourself

*Potty training...or maybe not*

A loss of personal bathroom privacy

*Choosing a preschool*

Hearing your child say a word you didn't know they overheard

*Lots of messes*

In not so many weeks you may discover an emerging two-year-old who is ready to keep showing you, **"I can do it."**

# Two-Year-Old

Still in the phase when nobody's on time, everything's a mess, and one eager toddler will insist, *"I can do it."*

### Expect to be late.

Maybe you had to wait for your toddler to "do it myself" (just try and stop them). Or maybe they impressively filled a clean diaper just as you got into the car. Whatever the reason, this phase will make even the most punctual adult miss the mark occasionally.

### Look forward to a few fashion statements.

Expect a few mismatched outfits, magic marker tattoos, sticker collages, and other various states of creative expression. In this phase, you will choose not only your battles, but also which messes will just have to be tolerated.

### Their struggle for independence has begun.

Your first clue might be your toddler's three new favorite words: "me," "myself," and "I." Just remember, by letting them do some things "myself," they're not only learning new skills, they're also developing the confidence they need in order to move to the next phase.

# The Phase Timeline

## About the Timeline

The one thing that is true across every phase is that your child will change—and so will your role as a parent. The phase timeline is a visual to help you see the progression through their first 18 years. Reference it over time to remember where you have been and to get an idea of where you are heading.

## About the Curve

Your child will also experience different levels of intensity across the phases. Watch for where the line rises to know when your child may be experiencing more developmental intensity. Whenever that seems overwhelming, this timeline is a reminder that it's just a phase.

*Remember: We haven't met <u>your</u> kid. This timeline is just what's true for a lot of kids.*

**Preschool** → **Your role is to embrace their physical needs.**

↓

**Elementary School** → **Your role is to engage their interests.**

↓

**Middle School** → **Your role is to affirm their personal journey.**

↓

**High School** → **Your role is to mobilize their potential.**

# The Preschool Phase

**Your Role →**

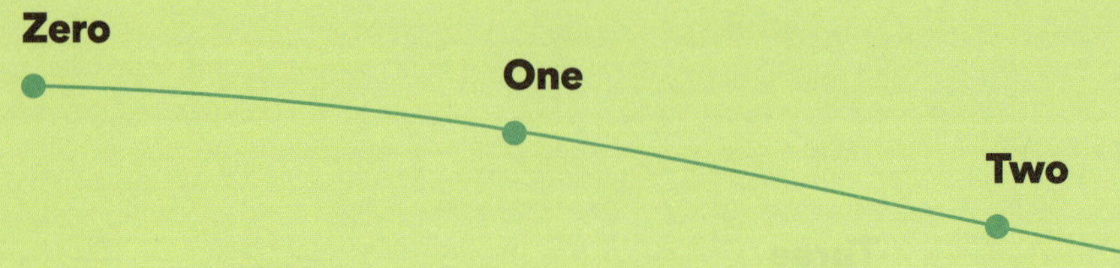


| **New Baby** | **One-Year-Old & Two-Year-Old** |
|---|---|
| **Wants to know...** | **Wants to know...** |
| Am I safe? | Am I able? |
| **So...** | **So...** |
| Establish trust. | Develop their confidence. |

**Thinks Like →**

A preschooler thinks like an artist, so engage with their senses.

**Motivated By →**

A preschooler is motivated by safety, so respond consistently.

**Three**

**Four**

## Three-Year-Old & Four-Year-Old

**Wants to know...**

Am I okay?

**So...**

Cultivate their self-control.

# It's just a phase,
# so don't miss it.

# SECTION 5.   NOTES

*Parenting Your One-Year-Old*

# SECTION 5.    NOTES

*Parenting Your One-Year-Old*

# SECTION 5.    NOTES

# Be the parent you want to be with Parent Cue.

We believe in every parent's ability to be the parent their child needs. Good parenting takes on many forms!

Parent Cue is here to cue you with what you need, when you need it—curated content, weekly inspiration, free resources, products, and more—so you are equipped to be the parent you want to be.

**Get started → parentcue.org**

# Parent smarter, not harder.

Make the most of everyday moments on the go. Download the free Parent Cue app to get weekly cues and content to connect with your kid in every phase from New Baby to Twelfth Grade—available for iOS and Android. Weekly phase content also available with an in-app subscription.

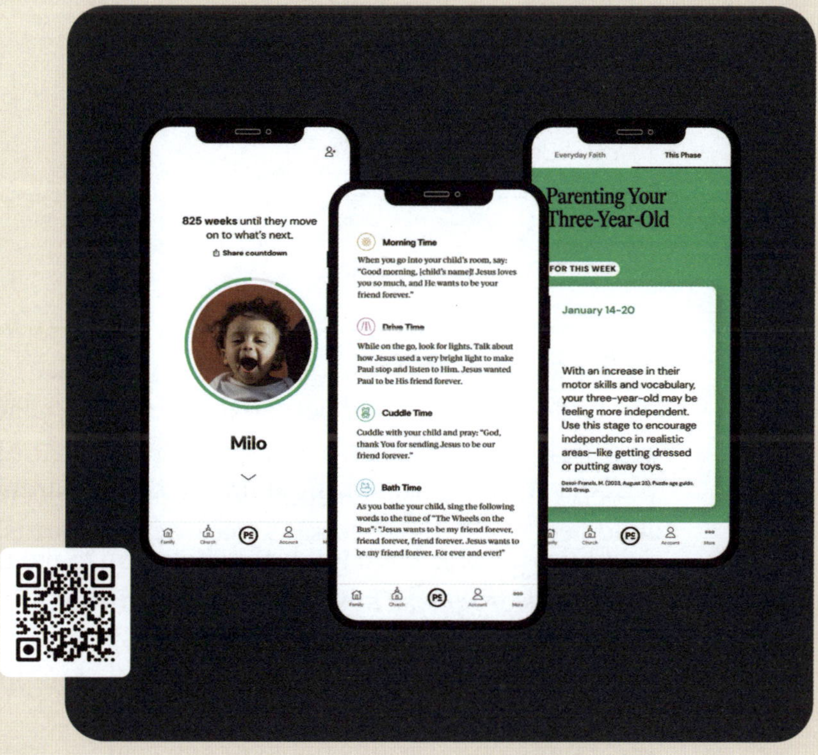


**Download now → parentcue.org/app**

# Ready for the next phase.

These guides are the core product of the Phase Project—a synthesis of personal experience, academic research, and gatherings of leaders and educational experts from across the child development spectrum.

Just like this one, each guide will help you make the most of every phase in your child's life through:

① What is changing about your kid
② The six things your kid needs most
③ Four conversations to have each year
④ Rhythms and responses
⑤ What's next

## A guide for every phase.

This guide is one of an eighteen-part series, so you can follow your parenting journey across every phase from New Baby to Twelfth Grade.

| **Preschool Phase** | **Elementary School Phase** | **Middle School Phase** | **High School Phase** |
|---|---|---|---|
| **New Baby**<br>The "I need you now" Phase | **Kindergartner**<br>The "Look at me!" Phase | **Sixth Grader**<br>The "Who Cares" Phase | **Ninth Grader**<br>The "This is Me Now" Phase |
| **One-Year-Old**<br>The "I can do it" Phase | **First Grader**<br>The "Look at me!" Phase | **Seventh Grader**<br>The "Who's Going?" Phase | **Tenth Grader**<br>The "Why not?" Phase |
| **Two-Year-Old**<br>The "I can do it" Phase | **Second Grader**<br>The "Sounds like fun!" Phase | **Eighth Grader**<br>The "Yeah… I Know" Phase | **Eleventh Grader**<br>The "Just Trust Me" Phase |
| **Three-Year-Old**<br>The "Why?" Phase | **Third Grader**<br>The "Sounds like fun!" Phase | | **Twelfth Grader**<br>The "What's Next?" Phase |
| **Four-Year-Old**<br>The "Why?" Phase | **Fourth Grader**<br>The "I've Got This" Phase | | |
| | **Fifth Grader**<br>The "I've Got This" Phase | | |

Shop now → phaseguides.com